Beauties in Flowers
REVERSE
Coloring Book

This book belongs to:

....

....

....

Inspiration

There are no rules! But you can try some of these ideas.

- flowers
- monsters
- faces
- tracing colors
- dotted lines
- dashed lines
- dots
- lines
- wiggly lines
- black lines
- white lines
- petals
- stacking shapes
- leave it
- rounded shapes
- circles
- shading
- double lines
- spirals
- leaves
- loops
- stacked lines
- squares
- bubbles
- stars
- hearts
- triangles
- color lines
- thick lines
- wobbly lines

You can use any tool you like. Experiment with different thicknesses, textures and colors. Find out which one you like the most. You`ll be suprised by the effect.

Sample drawing

www.ingramcontent.com/pod-product-compliance
Lightning Source LLC
Chambersburg PA
CBHW082356220526
45470CB00008B/2763